THE

FAST

MEMORY

Remember Everything, Learn Fast - With
Exercises and the Best Step-By-Step
Memorization Techniques

Disclaimer

Contents

INTRODUCTION

Remembering things can be one of the easiest things to accomplish; but ironically, it can also turn out to be one of the most difficult tasks. Before we go into the matter, let us first examine the scenario of Derek and Chelsea, my classmates in Fountain High School in California. Derek, as we all knew him, was studious, and he had the custom of going to the library regularly to read. Chelsea, by contrast, used to study at her own pace. However, it was discovered that Chelsea could remember things faster than Derek. In fact, sometimes, Derek would go on a reading spree for hours and yet remember little or nothing, while Chelsea, reading at her pace, was a high-flyer. Now, Derek was not a slow learner; he just could not remember things easily. Of course, as high school kids, we joked about Derek, while we celebrated Chelsea. We left high school, and the last thing I heard of Derek was that he had not gone to college because his grades were too poor, and his parents were not ready to waste their money in any case.

I am sure that anyone reading this story would be sad for Derek, right? Oh, lest I forget Chelsea, the last I heard, she is now an investment banker at Merrill Lynch. Back to Derek: it is evident that his story is sad? That is what not remembering things can do. Remembering things has long been one of the basic characteristics of humans. Why? This is because the human brain is made up of the cerebrum, or the seat of intelligence. Without the ability to remember things, humans would more or less be dummies.

After establishing the fact that remembering things is very important, something man cannot do without it, it is important to note that the rate at which people remember things varies. Memory affects the rate at which people learn things, and it may be impaired by health issues or sometimes hereditary problems. If their parents and ancestors have problems, the offspring are likely to have issues remembering things.

Talking about remembering things, note that in every human life, there are times when one is not going to remember things. But don't despair. As you read on, you will see what you can do.

How to Remember Anything

When talking about how to remember things, we cannot limit it to one aspect; there are many branches involved on the memory tree. Let us then examine these aspects and how each one helps.

HOW TO MEMORIZE EVERYTHING

While trying to memorize things, there are basic things to do.

- **The Method of coupling Words:**
  There are methods to the process of coupling of words. However, the methods all entail coupling concepts you are trying to remember. Doing this facilitate will the memorizing. How then do you do it?

  The Coupling of Numbers works with a particular set of numbers using a mental image. This is the reason why a lot of passwords and codes are anniversary dates, birthdays, and other things with personal meaning. If, for instance, you are trying to remember your laptop password (say it's 12041998), it's easy if April 12, 1998 is your birthday. To recall your password, simply think of your birthday.

In addition, you could use a cartoon or unusual picture to remember a cogent point you need to recall. For instance, if you're trying to remember Obama's victory date as a US president, picture Americans going in multitudes to vote for him and a calendar page. The coupling of Americans voting for Obama and the calendar will help you surely remember his victory date.

- **Endeavor to Picture things**
  In being intentional about remembering things, ensure you concentrate on picturing things as they occur. Definitely, in picturing things, you will focus on the important facts. If you are trying to remember a quote, for instance, concentrate on picturing the words of the part of that book you're reading and the style in which the quote is written. You thus create a pictorial aid helps you remember the exact words.

- **Use Prompting Implements**
  Some things are difficult to accomplish vis the coupling or picturing method. This necessitates employing a different method, called prompting implements. There are diverse implements one can employ. However, some work better than others. Join me on this ride:

a) Prompters can be pivotal for recalling the spelling of words. How can you form your own prompters? Compose a rhyme or anything that works for you. Just make sure to use a word for each letter. For instance, to remember your dad's birthday, you might recall the song, forever young by Alfa Ville.

b) Also, in trying to remember things, you can employ acronyms. You take the first letter of each word and change it to an acronym of your choice that makes sense. You can use MR NIGER D for life processes (Movement, Respiration, Nutrition, irritability, Growth, Excretion, Reproduction and Death).

c) You can use a phrase that does not make sense to remember a sequence. This method of remembering things is used a lot in mathematical formulas. For instance, My Very

Eyes May Just See Under Nine Planets is used to remember the nine planets (Mercury, Venus, Earth, Mars, Jupiter, Saturn, Uranus, Neptune, and Pluto.

d) Also, you can make up small rhymes to recall the desired material.

- **Create Stories**

  When trying to remember a collection of pictures, for example, on product descriptions, for example, you can create a short story. The short story fixes the pictures in your mind and you can recall them later. An example, cook up a story to remember coconuts, pears, mangoes, and oranges, among other things. Invent a story of a coconut being a bad person and the pears, mangoes, and oranges being good. The mangoes, pears, and oranges then have to collaborate to conquer the bad and strong coconut. This way, there is a very high likelihood that you will not forget the various types of fruit.

- **Change the way objects are arranged in your house**

  A very effective way to recall things is to change the way you arrange your house and moving them somewhere less obvious. If for example, you change the place of a piece of furniture, you will definitely remember where you put it as a deliberate act.

- **Be really interested in what you're learning**
  Now, this is very important for learners. It was discovered that those who have an interest in what they are learning tend to remember it better and more quickly. It is the same with relationships, if we are attracted to someone, we tend not to forget the specific things about them. If you really want to remember things, you have to be interested in the subject.

- **Try to increase the sharpness of your vision**
  If you want to remember things well, this is a potent method. Start out by practicing at parties. Look at five people and memorize their facial features to remember who they are. For instance, you can see that Jerry has big lips and Craig has small ears. Write down the items to be recalled. This worked for me when I was learning my first twenty elements. When you list out facts in writing, it increases the rate at which you remember them. You are not writing things down because you want to learn them; you are doing it because you want to actively remember them. It must be stressed that the best way to know a thing is to continually practice it.

- **Try Studying Mostly in the afternoon**

  Any one reading this might say that the time to assimilate material is in the morning or the evening. However, studies have shown that the best time for study is in the afternoon when one is most alert.

- **Get Sufficient Sleep**

  If you really want to remember something, don't neglect your sleep. This does not just mean sleeping at night after studying, but also the day before a big test. Furthermore, if you are having an interview the next day, do not stay up all night. Do a bit of studying in the daytime and sleep through the night so your brain stores and understands the processed data. What measures ensure quality sleep? The first thing is to switch off every electronic device around you at least twenty-five minutes before bed. It has been discovered that most people who complain of lack of sleep are most often obsessed with their electronic devices, particularly their phones. The thing about these electronic devices is that the light they emit is dangerous and deters good sleep, making the brain stressed and less productive. Never joke about the recommend hours a human being must sleep: eight hours! A lot of people who have difficulty remembering things take these recommended hours for granted.

For school-age children, there are ways to remember most anything:

- **Never try to do many things at the same time**

  When aiming to remember something, you have to have undivided attention. In addition, don't make things complicated for yourself. Why do people put a pen in a place and then forget it almost at the same minute? The reason is that at the time, they were probably thinking of someone, an undone household chore, among other possibilities. What then can you do to ensure your undivided attention? First, if you are studying and striving to recall things for school, concentrate on those things and avoid divergent thoughts such as your friend's pool party. Random, divergent thoughts are of no benefit and they cloud the brain.

- **Avoid disturbances coming from inside**

  Did you know your brain can disturb you? Yes! You're probably amazed, but it is true. Look at this scenario: you are trying to read but your brain is not quite concentrating on the material. Rather, it is focusing on your friend's pool party. How then do you conquer these disturbances from within? Well, you can set a reward for yourself if you conquer the distraction. You can say that for not obsessing on your friend's pool party, you will give yourself cream yogurt. Next, get a pad of paper and jot your divergent thoughts. In so doing, you will quickly see what is hindering your focus. Seeing a list of your thoughts will make you realize how unimportant they are.

- **Avoid disturbances around you**
  When trying to remember anything, it is advised to get away from your immediate surroundings. That is, away from people or things that can distract you. It could be your pets, friends, siblings or neighbors. How can you do this? The first step to get rid of disturbances by finding a quiet place that is well ventilated and properly lit. In this type of place, you are more likely to stay awake and alert. Second, make sure that when in this specific place of study, all you are going to do there is study. When trying to remember something, do not do anything other than concentrating on it.

If you discover that after taking the two measures mentioned above, you are still unable to work and retain, take a short break. However, this break does not mean that you involve yourself in things that won't encourage you to come back to the task at hand. What you should do is just take a short walk so that your brain is refreshed, after which you can return to studying again.

- **After each paragraph of your reading material, do a summary in the margins** Write a short summary of every paragraph in the margins if you want to remember the material. It not only boosts the ability to retain things, but it also juggles the memory when reading over complex things. How do you summarize in margins? Write down the major points of you are reading so you can jog the memory later when needed.

When trying to recollect things for a long period, this is what to do.

- **Engage in body exercises**
  There is a major relationship between mental and bodily health. Therefore, optimizing the health of your body will help maintain the health of your mind and boost memory. This is what you should do: jog for ten kilometers each day. It may be tedious at first, but you will soon get used to it. If you do this consistently, it will improve your mental faculties in the long run. Jogging is not the

only exercise you can engage in; there is a whole lot you could do to optimize your mental health o make you remember better.

- **Exercising your mind is very important**
  It has been discovered that exercising the mind helps prevent loss of memory and boosts its ability altogether. What stresses your brain are the things that make you tired and make you crave rest. Mostly, these things deal with mathematical problems, reading large volumes of materials, among other things. How then do you exercise your mind? You can start by writing to cram a poem every three weeks. What does this do? It is a very efficient trick and pivotal in improving the rate at which you remember. Therefore, memorize the Phoenix today!

- **Try to say the things you are trying to remember out loud**
  This actually works well for those who forget at a very fast rate. For instance, maybe you forgot whether you have turned on the water heater. If this is your case, saying the things you are trying to remember out loud will help a lot. If you want to recall a date or the time of an action, say the

date or time out loud. If it is an upcoming birthday party, say the date out loud several times so it will stick. If it is a person's name, just keep saying the name over and over. By doing this, there is no way you're not going to remember the name, time or date when the time to recollect comes,

- **Don't let anything escape your notice**
  What this means is that you have to be observant. When trying to remember things, never let any important detail escape your notice. Keep your nose to the ground in order to remember important details. Ensure that you observe people's faces, the time of important actions, where you have put things and so on. How do you do this? As a scene or event is unfolding, make sure you look intently at what is happening at that point in time. You can then close your eyes and register all the details of that event or scene in your mind. A consistent practice of this skill over time will ensure that in no time, you will have a sharper recollection ability. Apart from looking at people's faces and then closing your eyes, you can also use photographs. Take a look at the picture and turn it over, then try to recollect the details. If you succeed, do it with another picture until you become proficient at it.

- **This might seem funny, but you really need to eat right to remember right**

  It has been discovered through research that some foods you eat will boost your memory in the long run. If you are really intentional about remembering things better, eat foods that contain antioxidants and Omega-3 Fatty acids. These foods are known to boost recollection ability. They include spinach, broccoli, and salmon, among other foods. It has been proved that foods containing trans-fats, like red meat and margarine, also contain cholesterol that blocks the brain's blood vessels and can cause a permanent or partial stroke. When the cholesterol gets into the brain's blood vessels, it deprives them of oxygen; and this can tamper with normal reasoning and memory. How do you eat good food? Eat four to five meals in the daytime instead of three solid ones. You are probably wondering why this is beneficial, right? It prevents unstable sugar levels hinder the proper functioning of the brain.

THE PHENOMENON OF FORGETTING THINGS

Forgetting things is one of the signs that human beings are imperfect. It is perhaps the most telling sign of our imperfection. It is a known fact that we forget a lot of what we read, watch and face in the world today. This is not to say that we do not remember things at all, but it is evident that forgetfulness is an obstacle that bests most of us. Faulty memory happens to everyone. There's always the possibility of losing your car keys. You leave a party and soon after you forget the guests' names. You're worried, right? Do not get worked up. No one has a hundred percent perfect memory. Human memory is quirky. There are times when we think we remember everything, but almost immediately, we discover that we do not remember accurately at all.

Scientists have conclusive proof of why we forget things. The established fact is that people forget things in different ways. Just look at how we remember things. We see some pictures, for example, and feel we know everything about them. However, this is more complicated than we think. Pictorial images are stored in what is called visual memory. Our minds use them to recollect the face of someone we've just met. Memories of what you had for lunch are stored in visual short-term memory. While this is being stored, the brain gets busy performing other tasks. We need to ask ourselves, why do humans forget things? Aren't our brains a repository of memory?

> The most credible reason is that in our world today, humans focus on many things and not on recalling events.

Memory is vital in defining who we are. However, it has been noted that humans do not approach new events in the world with the goal of recalling them. Instead, we have the aim of enjoying, negotiating, condemning, loving or arguing. All these things do not pertain to recall; they have to do with comprehending.

There are a lot of things we do that show the purpose of comprehending alone. Memory research has placed too much emphasis on memory rather than recollecting. Instead of placing an emphasis on a lot of areas, we focus only on one -- studying for exams, for example. Situations of focus for recall are actually minute. In our everyday lives, we do not concentrate on everything we do; we focus on performing actions.

Furthermore, it is clear that we live or lives attending to the present alone and neglect the past, even though it is the framework that shapes the present. By the same token, if we walk into a room and forget the reason we are there, it should not come as a shock. This is because when we decide to walk to a place to do something, we are only focused on accomplishing the action and not remembering the action to be carried out.

> Another reason we forget things is that as humans, it helps us forget the pains and upsets of life. After a heartbreak, death of a parent or perhaps one's partner, or maybe a disturbing occurrence, a lot of us discover that as time goes on, the pain becomes dull. However, it is not the time on the clock that makes the pain go away. Once clear emotional details tend to become less visible amidst on-going daily experience. The pain becomes dull and reduced in concentration.

Recently, it has been discovered that the cannabinoid neurotransmitters in our brains show the importance of both the past and the present on memory. These neurotransmitters increase the impact of the things we undergo through sense experience and remove the blockage of memory, putting us in the moment of perception and taking us away any memories that might unearth pain in us.

> ## It has been discovered that our brains select what they want to recollect

It was discovered that forgetting is an important factor in recollecting what is vital. Our memories are usually spot on for our needs at a certain point in time in order to recollect the details of an event and to retain specific visuals.

> ## Forgetting things enhances recollecting

Forgetting data that has been processed has a positive side. In fact, there are instances when forgetting details helps one to learn. For instance, in learning a new language, forgetting helps momentarily suppress the details of your native language. It is also important to note that those good at forgetting details or processed data are those who are good at recollecting vital information when needed.

THE SCIENCE BEHIND REMEMBERING ANYTHING

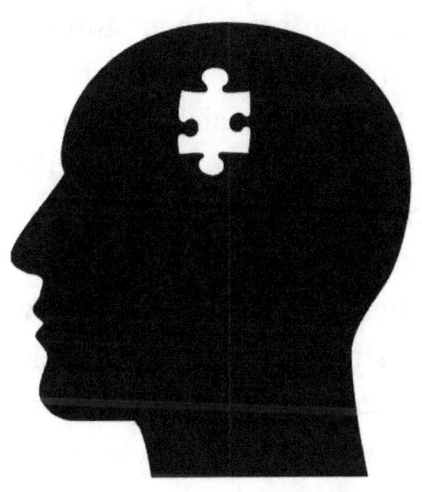

Essentially, remembering things is very scientific. As laymen, we all want to believe that remembering things is normal. However, research and science prove that in remembering things, there are a lot of scientific processes that the brain has to go through.

Let's first begin with how memory works. The first aspect of memory is encoding. When you notice a thing, text or anything in particular, the brain receives sound, images, and other sensory details and stores them. How then do we remember these things the brain has perceived? Extensive research shows us that the likelihood of recalling something is higher if we encode it by attaching meaning. For instance, if you relate Antarctica to its extreme icy weather, you are encoding Antarctica with meaning.

After encoding, the brain then stores the processed data in different parts of its structure. The nerve cells in the brain transfer signals. We could say that they relate to one another. It is when this process is completed that a memory is created. You may wonder after all these long processes, how our brains then retrieve the memories stored? It is the work of nerve cells in the brain. The brain has both long-term and short-term memory. For instance, what you eat for dinner is a memory that the brain can let go of immediately after the action is complete, but the brain will surely not let go of your birthdate unless senility has set in.

After storing memory, be it short-term or long term, when the brain wants you to remember, it consults the pathway created when the memory was made. It has been discovered that a recurrent remembrance of details makes these pathways stronger.

Seeing briefly how humans remember things, it is important to also note that a memory cannot be exactly the same as the one recorded when the real event happened. This is because memories are not static; they get mixed up with older memories. It is clear that human memory is rich because it is complex and is tangled up with a lot of factors.

TECHNIQUES OF REMEMBERING ANYTHING

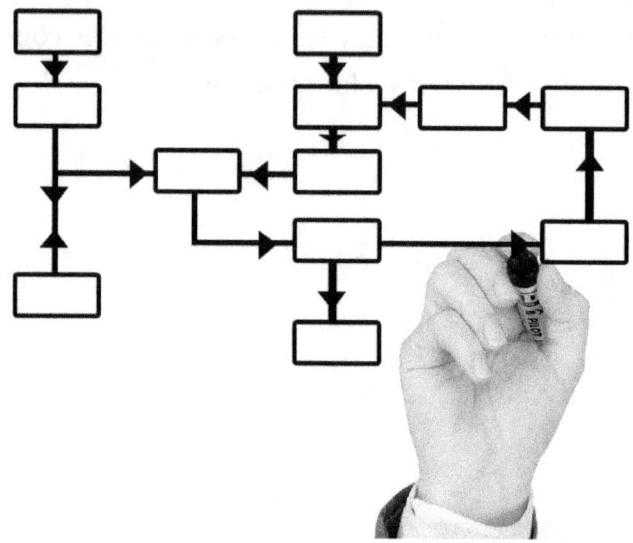

We often find people who have given up on remembering things. They claim that nothing they do helps them remember. However, this is a misconception; remembering things is a skill that can be groomed and developed to function optimally. This is a fact! Those who have wonderful memories are not different from anyone else. All they do is use different methods to allow their minds to recall things like equations, dates, lists, tasks, or a new language among other things. If you use the correct methods, you will soon be proficient at recalling most anything. My advice is that you sit back and open your mind to these ground-breaking techniques.

- **Some might not like this; however, it is recommended to play video games.**
  Contrary to the negative perception of video games, research says they help us form better memories as one advances in age. Specifically, games that are tri-dimensional do this better. Playing some video games like Super Mario consistently increase the brain's grey matter. As you play games and have fun, you develop your brain's capability to recall thing efficiently.

- **If you are going to a room or a place, picture what you want to take from that room or place before you go there.**
  There's something about going into a room or passing through a door that changes memory short-term and does not help us remember the exact reason we are going there. What do we do? The solution is to picture the reason before you leave the place you are in. This way, the probability of recalling what you want to get from or do that room is very high. This also relates to the ever-changing digital world. Make sure that before you open a new tab on your screen, you

visualize the reason why you're doing it. Do not just surf the internet meaninglessly without remembering the purpose. In fact, for most people who open new tabs without knowing the reason, they remember why much later or not at all. For me, I have been using a method that has been working very well. For instance, I usually forget where I put my running shoes after returning from the gym; what I do now is to focus on the part of my room where I put the removed shoes. This way, the next time I need them, all I need to do is picture where I had put them before and I definitely remember.

- **Chunking is a must-learn!**
  You must learn how to break things down into bits if you really want to remember anything. It has been discovered that our short-term memory cannot store a lot of things at one time. According to scientists, it can store a minimum of four and a maximum of seven things. The chunking method gets one out of this limited capability. What do you do? You simply segment different items from a larger whole.

- **Music has a lot of power; so use it!**
  Numbers and names are forgotten easily. However, we tend not to forget the words of

rhymes taught in primary school. If, for example, you want to learn the lexis of another language, use musical cues or songs.

- **Endeavor to learn things and pay attention to your healthcare**
It is no longer news that one of the things that promotes memory loss is age. As we grow older, our memories begin to deteriorate. However, learning new skills and paying attention to your all-around health goes a long way in improving memory. You should reduce stress and exercise both your body and your brain.

- **Always practice consistently**
In order to remember things more accurately, three things to note are: you must be motivated, observant and employ accurate mechanics. A lot of people forget because they are not really paying attention. Accurate mechanics is all about finding the precise and unique way to remember things that works best for you. Once you have done this, the next step is to keep using this method consistently. Practicing means reviewing the names or details of people you encounter consistently. There's a great possibility that over time, remembering things, in general, is not going to be such an issue for you any longer.

- **Interact with people differently to help you recognize their faces**

  Have you ever been at a party and you meet someone who had been introduced to you before? Just when you're about to pronounce the person's name, you totally forget it? Don't get all worked up about it; it's not senility. The problem is that our brains have a way of failing us, sometimes at the most important times. It is due to the limited capability of basic working memory. In spite of memory inadequacies, if one creates a relation between the name and the person in question, it's very likely that we'll never forget the name.

- **Make use of memory palaces**

  It has been discovered that the most effective mnemonic device is the memory palace. A lot of people highly skilled at remembering things are die-hard practitioners of the memory palace. It has its origin in Ancient Greece. Here's how it works. The most important idea of the method is to relate pieces of processed data that one wishes to recall with segments you know very well. One place you are conversant with might be your office.

Start with picturing oneself walking through the office and recalling every detail you can. Employ all your sensory organs. Relate each item you want to recall with a particular object or part of your office. For instance, if you are trying to learn a new language, you may want to store all things related to weather in your file cabinet. Relating items you want to recall with a real physical space is pivotal for the brain to file critical things for easy recall. Memory palaces have several purposes: to recall faces, languages, academic material, among other things.

THE FEYNMAN TECHNIQUE

This technique works best for remembering processes and conceptual knowledge. To memorize "hard data" such as numbers or names, you might want to consult the following chapters instead.

Richard Phillips Feynman was an American physicist and Nobel Price winner of the year 1965. He participated in the Manhatten Project, introduced the concept of nanotechnology and he has been credited with pioneering the field of quantum computing. But did you know that he was also a brilliant teacher? In fact, he developed a method for remembering complex processes and was thus able not only to memorize but also explain difficult stuff to his students. The basic idea of his technique was to try to explain what you need to learn to others (even if there is nobody in the room). See, if you can explain stuff, you understand it! Also, by trying to explain problems or processes, you will quickly identify your problem areas as points in your explanation where you are stuck and don't find the right words.

In short, Feynman's method works as follows:

a. Write down the name of the problem/process or concept you want to learn. This helps you to get the (very) big picture into your head.
b. In your own words, explain the process or concept to yourself as if you were speaking to a child. Use examples and step-by-step explanations. Write that down. In this step, you will identify what you do not understand about the things you want to learn.
c. Review what you have written down in step b. For anything you were not able to explain well enough, research or review the source material, find more examples, etc.

d. Review again what you have written down in step b, but now focus on areas where you have used complex language and difficult words. Try to find easier phrases that describe the same thing. The easier your explanation is, the easier you will be able to fully remember it.

e. If you found some stuff to re-work on during steps c and d, you might want to go back to step b and do it again.

When explaining the process or concept, try to explain it step-by-step. Use examples and maybe metaphors.

REMEMBERING NUMBERS

As we all know, numbers are quintessential in human life. Be it adding, subtracting, multiplying or dividing, when it comes to calculation, numbers are key. When trying to remember numbers, the best thing to do is use prompters. When you want to remember numbers and use a prompting list system, it becomes easy.

In almost everything task in life, we cannot do without numbers. Of course, numbers are not easy to remember because they cannot be substantiated. Here is another example from my personal life: five years after my family moved to Honolulu, I couldn't recollect our ZIP code. It has been discovered by neurosurgeons that if a thing does not have a meaning, it becomes very difficult to recollect it. For instance, if the word "sheep" is mentioned and you have reared or seen a sheep, it will make all the old memories stir up. The problem is that a lot of humans do not have an emotional connection to numbers.

From the mathematical perspective, a lot of those skilled at recollecting numbers have great associated meanings with them. Those who study mathematics have a strong advantage because they are regularly exposed to numbers. If for instance, you bring up the number 2468, the chances are very high that a typical mathematician will sort it into four digits that can be divided by two.

- **Long numbers**

  In order to remember long numbers, you can use the prompting system which has proven to be the most effective. At a simple level, single numbers can be stored at each stop, using this effective system. For longer and more advanced numbers, you can use the major system. When you use these simple techniques, you should be able to store a hundred-digit number. In doing this, make sure you don't rush.

- **Learn the rules of the phonetic system**

  One method of remembering numbers is known as the phonetic system. In this system, you build relations between individual numbers and a sound or word. It is a known fact that you will remember more accurately when you use words you have constructed from a group of numbers you are trying to remember.

- **Sense organs**

  The sense organs, particularly the ears, are very efficient when it comes to remembering numbers. This is how it works;

  a) Picture the number and write it down several times so as to store it in your memory bank. Better yet, you can make a very clear image of the number you want to remember. For example, create a picture of 2594 printed on a cardboard. There is no way you're going to forget the number!

  b) Repeat the number to yourself. At first, it may be difficult to do this; recalling 2594 cannot be substantiated. However, it will be very easy to remember the sound of 2594.

- **Change numbers into words to remember them**

A very effective way to remember numbers is to give every number a letter. L=22, M=23, N= 24, O=25 and so on. By using this method, 123 turns into ABC. The letters, ABC, do not make a lot of sense so you can turn it into a crossword. You can turn it into **A**ll **B**asic **C**ars. The next time you want to remember 123, you just remember **A**ll **B**asic **C**ars and then change the first letter of the words back to the numbers. However, if you think you might forget **A**ll **B**asic **C**ars, you can change it to anything you feel will jar your memory immediately. For example, say you want to recall the password of your personal computer. You can picture your computer as **B**ig **E**ggs **S**cattered **T**oday.

- **The image assigning method**
  When using this method, you can apportion an image to every number you are trying to remember. Look at the numbers below.

10 = Glass

11= Crate

12= Plates

13= Fork

14= Pringles

15= Mule

16= Catfish

17= Grass

18= Trigger

19= Boat

These number equivalents are not a joke; try to cram all that have been itemized and if you find that you cannot still recollect the numbers, then change them to something you can recollect better. For instance, if you want to recollect the address of your friend's company, which is 1248, you can picture a dog (1) running after a thief (2) catching the thief (4) and tearing him to shreds (8). You can also use other assigners to indicate the numbers you are trying to remember. It can get quite creative and fun.

- **Employ the major memory technique**
  This is an in-depth look into the major memory technique as a way of remembering numbers. This

method is very effective but is a little bit intricate, as it involves a lot of processes. How do you go about it? Every number is given a consonant sound based on the following factors:

0= s, z soft-c ("z" is the first letter of zero)

1= t ("t" is similar to a 1 with a line through it)

2 = n ("n" has two bars)

3 = m ("m" has three bars)

4 = r ("r" is the letter of four)

5 = L ("L" is Roman numeral for 50)

6 = j, sh, ch, soft-g ("g" is 6 rotated 180degrees)

7 = k ("k" looks like two 7s rotated and pasted together)

8 = f, v ("f" written in cursive has two loops similar to 8)

9 = p, b ("p" and "b" looks like 9 in different angles)

This is how this technique operates. The consonant sounds of the numbers are set and vowels are added. When this has been successfully done, groups of words, phrases, and sentences are formed.

- **Create Associations**
  It is a known fact that some numbers have semantic meaning for us; they could be birthdates, anniversaries, memorials or a host of other things. What's the secret to recalling these numbers? From research, it has been discovered that the secret to remembering these numbers is to find relations between the numbers and any memories of the numbers that are firmly rooted in your brain. It has also been recommended that if you do not find a relating number for a word, move on to the next one to spur the remembrance and use it to connect the numbers together.

- **Segment large numbers into smaller bits**
  An average person can hold about seven unrelated units of processed data at once in a single memory. However, by segmenting or chunking the items into smaller bits, you can increase your ability to remember astronomically. You're probably worrying how this works? Let's put it into practice: try remembering 56781234672. It is a string of eleven separate numbers and most

likely it will be difficult to recall. However, if you can find two sensible dates in the sequence, recalling the numbers will be no problem because you would have segmented them into smaller bits.

Exercise: The math game

A common exercise amongst experts incorporates a simple math challenge:

a. Choose a random 3-digit number
b. Choose numbers to add and subtract
c. Add the number you chose in step b to the original 3-digit number. Repeat 3 times
d. Subtract the number you chose in step b from the result
e. Go back to step c and repeat 5 times
f. Go back to step a and chose a new 3-digit number

This will train not only your math skills. During the exercise, you will also have to remember a lot of things:

- The current result
- The number to add
- The number to subtract
- How often you have performed the addition

- How often you have performed the whole calculation

This exercise hides the memorization training in a nice little game of math.

Here is an example:

1. We chose 241 as our 3-digit-number
2. We chose the number 4 to add and the number 7 to subtract
3. Now we perform three additions:
   a. $241 + 4 = 245$
   b. $245 + 4 = 249$
   c. $249 + 4 = 253$
4. Now we perform the subtraction:
   a. $253 - 7 = 246$
5. The first cycle is complete. We start the second one by performing three more additions:
   a. $246 + 4 = 250$
   b. .....

Of course, you should not use pen and paper when performing this exercise!

You can vary the degree of difficulty by using 2-digit numbers or 4-digit numbers instead.

Try it **now** with a 2-digit number!

REMEMBERING NAMES

A person's name is the sweetest and most important sound in any language. It is a known fact that using a name one of the most efficient ways of creating a positive first impression or sealing an important business deal. It is near impossible to get a customer to buy your goods regularly if you cannot recollect their name. The thing about recollecting people's names is that it shows that they have a level of importance to you. On the flip side, if you tend to forget people's names or mistake them, it could be very dangerous for business and personal relationships. In business, a good first impression can have a long-lasting effect. In fact, research has shown that when you remember people's names, it shows how important they are to us.

It is difficult to demonstrate to a person that you care about their business if you're not mindful enough to take cognizance of their name. We only have trained memories. This means that memory is something you do, not something you automatically have. In terms of remembering names, it would be amiss not to do an in-depth discussion of why we forget names so easily.

WHY WE FORGET NAMES

The simplest answer to this question is that one is not always totally interested. It has been discovered that when people are motivated, they tend to recall things better. At times, learning names is a passing thing. It is not the case in all instances; there times when we really want to recollect names but just can't. It is like not recalling the person. A household name may escape your mind because it is not interesting. On the flip side, a rare name may be easy to identify but difficult to recall. Every name, rare or common, has to fight for a place in your already-crowded brain. Not only is the name worth remembering, but you are also recollecting the name in relation to a face. Even if your brain encodes the information correctly, you might not be able to review the processed data at will because you have a host of other things stored.

Who falls into this category? They are those who lose focus even when they are trying to make a good impression.

How to Remember Names

- **You have to be committed**

  You have to have a commitment to recall names; don't use the excuse that you do not have an excellent memory. It has been discovered that recalling someone's name has to do with a lack of application rather than a slow memory. Before going anywhere, continually remind yourself that you want to do your best to recall the names of all the people you meet that day.

  It is equally important that you are committed to the time you are introduced to a person. It has been discovered that more often than not, we view the time of introduction with levity as we feel there are more important things to come. Therefore, it comes as no surprise that after the introduction, we tend to forget the names. What do you do to prevent this? When meeting a person and being introduced, you have to be intentional enough to step up your curiosity and greet the person with the singular intent of listening actively to what he or she is saying.

- **Repetition of names is very important**

  What does repetition of names do? It helps keep the name you want to recall firmly rooted in your memory. You first have to use the name immediately, repeat it slowly, and, if possible, comment on the name, use it in conversation. In the event you are talking with someone for the first time, actively ask for their name. While looking at their face, repeat the name to yourself. It cannot be overemphasized that this makes the brain pin the name to the face, increasing the likelihood that you'll recollect the names the next time. It's like using your mental faculties to write the person's name on their face.

- **You must focus completely**

  It is a known fact that if you are distracted, you can't possibly recall a person's name. The first thing to do is focus on that name, then form an impression about it. you can't do this without first listening to the name. If at the end of four or five minutes, you cannot seem to recall the name, tell the person you have simply missed it. In fact, if you have a problem spelling the name, you can ask the person to spell the name out. After this, you can get an in-depth look into the person in question. The more clearly you look at facial features, the more likely you are to recall them. You can use all your senses to create the most profound impression of the person.

- **Try to form relations**
  Relate a person's face to an image the name implies. Shape the name into a characteristic of the person's face. In the event that you can't make an image, don't be sad. You have made an attempt to picture the name and have thereby solidified your memory. Linking the physical characteristics of a person to a created image will help fixate the memory.

  Let us imagine that a doughnut weighing a kilogram is spinning on the end of Mr. Baxter's nose. After this, imagine an old-fashioned wheel spanner under Mr. Trinco's prominent jaw. Then imagine some shea butter melting through Michelle's thick, black hair. If music or rhymes are more inclined to help you, then create a poem or a song as the case may be.

  For instance, "Greg has a coat, Drake has a car, everybody has a car. When you go to London, put on your coat and dance with your merry coat." If you are comfortable with instincts and feelings, try connecting the name of the person to the sound the person's name creates as you say it. For example, Becky is a stubborn girl, Shaw is a brilliant boy, and Paula is bossy.

It is worthy of note that this process is time-consuming. However, a judicious adherence to it will make you win the trust of a lot of people, who know that you are very conversant with their name.

- **Try to look at things, take snapshots and link them up**
  The brain loves to link things and connect them. Building on this ability, when someone tells you their name, it is very likely you will recollect it at a later time. Examine the name. Does it recall something that makes your head turn? Can you relate the person's hobby to their name? Get innovative in the way you picture things. For instance, let's say the name is Sonia Bush. The first thing is to take a "snapshot" of her face. Then you might imagine someone walking into a bush. It might not be feasible and realistic but that's exactly how you're going to remember the name. In addition, it is recommended when

encountering a person with a difficult name, ask
them to spell it.

- **Asides commitment, consistency is very
  important**

  Being consistent at anything at all is very
  important because it breeds proficiency. While
  starting the process and after observing the
  various methods of remembering people's names,
  it may seem unnatural at times. It is just like
  when you're trying to take up anything new. But,
  enough of the complaints and excuses; if you
  adhere strictly to these techniques, they will soon
  become a part of you and remembering people's
  names at a high rate will no longer be an issue.

- **Lastly, trust yourself**

  Never go around with the belief that you are bad
  at recalling names. You should not go about
  telling others this. When you do, you are sending
  a message that there is no hope for improvement.
  Furthermore, by telling people, they tend to be
  less empathetic toward you. Be committed to
  improving always: never tire at it! Consider the
  disgust you feel when someone says he/she is not
  good at names. Since you feel disgusted at such a

comment it should be a wake-up call for you that there's still more to be done to improve yourself. Do it today and don't slack!

REMEMBERING HISTORY AND HISTORICAL DATES

History is a part of our lives. History is what makes us understand our roots, our heritage and a whole host of other valuable things. In fact, without history, human beings will not have a past. It is important to note that history definitely has to do with dates. From birthdays to war dates, to records of deaths, they all pertinent. It would be catastrophic if someone forgets their history. It wipes out their roots, culture, and customs. When we think of history, we think of the brain as its storehouse. If someone loses his or her memory, they lose it all. The person's personality and character washes away. Anyone who has seen someone lose his memory knows it is one of the worst tragedies in life. The memory of a society is its common history. Once a society loses that, it has no common past nor purpose. History provides lessons that shape the way we make decisions, both individually and collectively. It strengthens us to face difficulties with long-term solutions. History also provides real-life views of how wicked human nature is and the mammoth effort needed to overcome it.

In addition, memory has to deal with recollecting processed data. For healthy individuals, remembering processed data is part of daily life. However, recollecting things such as historical names might be tasking. There are ways you can boost your memory to recall important names and dates.

- **Create a rhyme**

   Having processed data in a rhythmic pattern such as a poem can be pivotal to facilitate memory improvement in order for you to remember historical dates. Classical instances include the "Remember, remember the eleventh of September" rhyme that marks the 9/11 attack on the twin towers at the World Trade Center sponsored by Al-Qaeda. The processed data you need to recollect depends on the amount you want to recollect.

- **Use the Loci Technique**

  The technique of Loci deals with relating names, dates or things in a particular place. Citing an example, if you want to recollect the names of presidents in correct order, think about walking to the door of your office and seeing a dollar bill on the floor. What does this arouse in you? It's most likely the image of George Washington.

- **Engage different sense organs**

  In order to store information long term such as dates in history, use your different sense organs in screening the processed data. Read it and say it aloud. Try organizing the material in an orderly arrangement, be it alphabetic or chronological. You can then screen the information and store it in your long-term memory.

- **Do not do away with the method of association**

  Relating newly-processed data with others can help increase the way you remember dates from history. You can use images, ranging from the visual to sounds and smells, or prior facts that relate to the new data at hand. For instance, if you want to remember the name, Gregory Bush, you might visualize your uncle Gregory standing beside a bush. If you do this, there is no way you are going to forget the name. If you're trying to recollect the day that Aretha Franklin died, which is 2018, every time you think of that day, imagine an old woman singing the Amazing Grace hymn.

Furthermore, an effective use of one's body can be pivotal in remembering history and critical dates. It has been discovered that you can make very strong associations to recall dates. How do you do this? If you're trying to recollect how J.F Kennedy was assassinated, imagine that you're in your car, with the roof open, and are sitting in the back while your driver drives. You can arrange processed data to remember dates. You do it in any logical way because when it comes to remembering a set of processed data not logically joined together, it may be difficult. This is why consistent practice is vital; as you practice the dates you need to recall, find a viable way to group them. Set a deadline for yourself in your quest to remember them.

This process connects dates to each other. The more you put the dates you're trying to recollect in a meaningful context, the better will be your ability to remember them. Maybe you are trying to remember all the birthdays of your family members. You can draw a family tree and keep practicing day by day as you contemplate it.

- **Use flashcards**

  Another potent and effective way of remembering historical dates is to use flashcards. If flashcards are used in the right way, they can be of immense help. How do you do this?

  a) You can use a set of cards or an electronic flash program in which you document the date on one side of the card. Furthermore, you can give yourself a quiz by looking at the cards, shuffling them at random and using them to recollect the dates. You can go back and look at the significance of the dates later if needed.

  b) As you go through the cards, bring out the ones you can recollect first and repeat them to yourself. However, the ones you cannot remember should be attended to with great care, so that you leave no stone unturned

  c) Frequently practice with the flashcards. However, do not rush things in short bursts but slowly and accurately.

REMEMBERING PEOPLE AND FACES

People make up our world. But it is actually very easy to forget a face. Doing so shows you are not someone who values others. However, there's no need to get worked up yet; we have been configured in different ways. For some, no matter how hard you try, you may still not remember much. In fact, it is even possible that the person prescribing the best way to remember people's face will himself not be able to recollect them. This is because our brains sometimes play tricks on us.

The problem of facial recognition is a serious issue in the world today. It has been discovered that in middle-aged and older adults, close to a hundred percent have great difficulty recalling the faces of people they have just met. Some know the names but cannot put faces to them. Others can put a name to a face but cannot recall the face at all. When this happens, it can cause a lot of embarrassment and frustration. Incidences like this can end relationships that could have been blossoming. Thank goodness for science; there are now methods to prevent the embarrassment that comes with forgetting faces.

In remembering faces, these are the very helpful hints to follow:

- **Identify the person's special characteristics**
  It has been shown beyond a reasonable doubt that people find it easier to recall faces than names in general. Our brains like to assimilate pictorial things because we can relate to them. One way is to focus on special characteristics. First, take your time to look at the hairstyle, nose, complexion, and hairline among other physical features that are prominent. Afterward, you can pick out the most unique trait; for instance, Jerry's lips are big.

- **Use a visual cue to relate to the face**
  This method is quite engaging and interesting. On a first meeting with a person, create an odd visual cue. A veteran in the memory business will focus mainly on physical features. For instance, take a

lady named, "Hilary." The veteran might want to make an immediate association with Hilary Clinton because she has a similar body. This method may sound silly; in fact, we could say that it most certainly is. However, silliness is the point. The sillier it is, the more likely you will remember it.

- **Connect the face to the name**
  In order to link a person's name to the face, repeat it always. Whenever you are speaking to the person, make sure you use their name and consciously look at them. When both of you have left each other, link the face and name together. To recall names, using cue cards or a timetable may be beneficial. Also, form mental devices. Know that the more you relate a name to a face, the more you are likely to improve your memory. It is important because the features of the face will help you remember the name.

REMEMBERING VOCABULARY

gram... [...accordance... ...in a way... ...gram... such... ...gram... form... ...compos... ing a thing written or recorded (off... a certain way) (anagram, epigram, gram). [Greek gramma thing writ... **graminaceous** /ˌɡræmɪˈneɪʃəs/ a... or like grass. [Latin gramen grass... **graminivorous** /ˌɡræmɪˈnɪvərəs... feeding on grass, cereals, etc. **grammar** /ˈɡræmə(r)/ n. **1** the stu... rules of a language's inflections or means of showing the relation be... words. **2** observance or applicat... the rules of grammar (bad gramm...

It does not matter how good you are at grammar, if you are not empowered with words, you won't go far with your language skills. The lexis of language opens doors to new horizons and makes the art of learning fun. However, increasing the words you know is like a diet. You have to be intentional. In fact, everyone has a unique way of remembering vocabulary; there's no one-size-fits-all method. You have to find what works for you and make realistic and realizable goals.

However, there are some ways to recall more vocabulary.

- **Use mental shortcuts**

  A popular mental shortcut to remember vocabulary is mnemonics. They help you recall intricate concepts. For instance, you can create relations like windows and balconies. Also, you can come up with an acronym like **S**alt, **T**urmeric, **E**ggs, and **M**angoes if you want to remember what to get at the market. However, the only problem is that you first have to store the acronym in your brain.

- **Use words in context**

  A great deal of vocabulary advancement can be done when you put words into a context. It is not every time, but you will sometimes want to consult the dictionary. There are times when the context in which the words are used will help you recollect them accurately. Also, funny sentences can aid your vocabulary development.

- **Real-life experiences will help**

  Songs, movies, podcasts among other things will help you recollect words accurately. This is because they always have some relation to a real-life scene. Therefore, in your quest to learn new words, try to read books and watch movies and try to decode what unfamiliar words mean.

- **Find tools that work for you**
  Everyone has their way of recollecting things. Therefore, if you don't know the method that works for you, try all the methods you can from flashcards to video games, lists, etc. This applies for building and recalling vocabulary too. The recommended time is in the afternoon when you are alert and active.

- **Make sentences**
  The art of making sentences will definitely help you recall words in which learned before. Learning a word is one thing and remembering it is another. To allow the brain to remember the word, use it regularly in sentences. Go for twenty sentences showing diverse meanings of the words you are trying to recall.

- **Be patient with yourself**
  You do not become proficient at something new overnight. By virtue of this, you have to have a lot of patience as you gradually learn how to recall vocabulary.

REMEMBERING PLACES

We go to different places in the world. There are places we have been to and places we've not wanted to go. People who once visit a place often say they can never forget what it looks like in detail. In addition, there are people who determine where they are going in advance and seem to know all about it. It does not matter what it takes to get there: they will find a way, right? Some are simply oblivious and can hardly remember the features of the place immediately after leaving. This brings us to the pertinent question, how to remember places?

How to Remember Places

In remembering places, the first step is to have a fantastic sense of direction. You have to have some interest in the place you are going as well. You will soon begin to take cognizance of the direction of the streets or roads you are journeying through. You have to look at every aspect of the environs. After developing more interest, you will begin to note the key landmarks. A lot of people are too preoccupied to notice the main characteristics of the lands they visit. For those who want to recall these places, there are no strong memories. It is important to take note of all the things you encounter along the way. When traveling, take out a pencil and make a map of the area and jot down the distinctive features of all the objects along the way.

From the scientific perspective, the hippocampus has the responsibility of recalling the places we've been to. In the brain are geotags connected to certain memories. When they are activated, the memory arises. The hippocampus has a very pivotal role in the balancing of vital processed data from short-term to long-term memory. Research has proven that the latitudinal and memory functions of the hippocampus are universal. It is not impossible to forget where you parked your car. Here's how to recall where you parked it. After you park the car, don't come out of the car and go straight to your destination. Try to look around and take note of where you are. You have to find something that will make you recollect.

Did you park near an alley or dumpster? Hang on to something that makes you recollect the place. As you go on your journey, take snapshots of the area with your mind. Afterward, you can flashback to what you snapped. The process involves signals from all directions. You have to employ all your senses. How do you do this? Pay attention to smells or noises. The more you employ your senses, the stronger the memories of places will be. In addition, you have to make use of maps. If you are skilled at reading maps, put down directions and screen them with all your strength before you leave where you are.

When it comes to remembering addresses, you can use the techniques mentioned above. For instance, if you want to recollect Cottonwood Avenue, you can change 62 into moon (6 = M, 2= n, then add vowels). Then for Cottonwood, picture a big plank of wood with cotton all over (or cotton candy). See now how we relate things together.

If you want to recall a large number, for example 462, you can change the number to crane (4 = c, 6 =r, 2= e). It is important to note that while these techniques will help you recall things, different ones will produce optimal results.

REMEMBERING QUANTITIES

It is evident that there are a lot of things that people have difficulty remembering. Quantities are among them. Quantities may seem inconsequential; however, when someone makes a wrong measurement decision, it could have far-reaching consequences. If, for instance, you happen to be a baker and can't seem to remember the quantities for, say, a cake, you will make a bad or burned one.

What you should do is picture the amount of things you want to include in the mixture to get the perfect result. In doing a job that requires mixing things together, say the measurements out loud. In the end, you'll find that you won't mix the wrong items or amounts. In fact, you may discover a backup plan. For every item you quantify, set a part of that item aside. By doing this, you will picture with precision how much of that item has been added if eventually you are distracted from what you are currently doing.

MORE EXERCISES

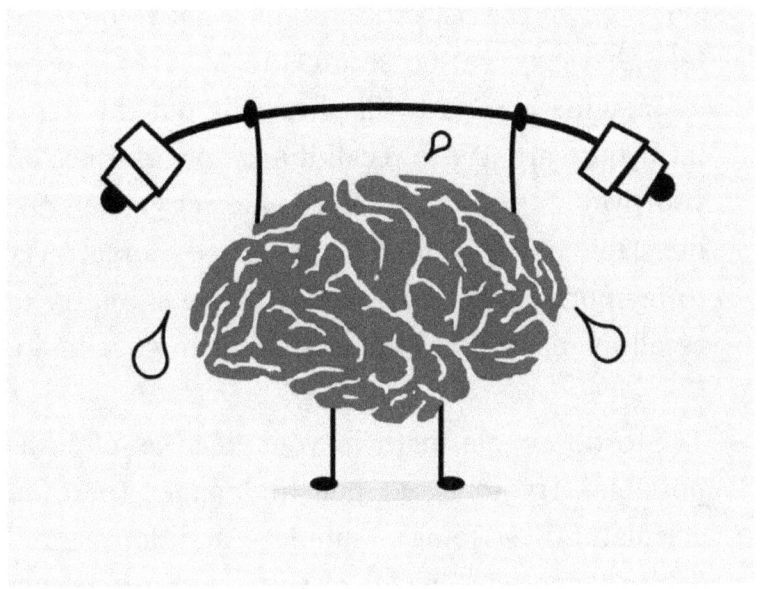

You can incorporate memorization exercises in your daily life. This way, you will get better and better a bit every day – without taking extra time. Just try, to remember stuff when you see it:

- Spoken words:
  You are walking, sitting in the train or having a snack? Try to listen to what people say around you. And then try to memorize what was being said. Try to recall spoken words a couple of minutes later. This is an easy way to improve your memory without spending extra time

- The list memo:
  Whenever you write a list, try to memorize it. A list of grocery items can be a perfect asset to you: Write down the list of items you want to buy and take that extra 30-60 seconds to try to memorize it. Imagine how you will physically put the items into your cart. Try to recall it a couple of times on your way to the store. Before entering, review the list: How many items did you already forget? Try to memorize them once again. In the store, try to recall as many items as possible from your mind.

- Try to do simple math in your head as often as possible. Try to avoid pen and paper (or even calculators). Doing simple additions and subtractions will challenge your memory as you would have to constantly remember intermediate results.

- Try to remember things in your daily life. This applies to potentially a lot of things: Your bus schedule, how much you pay for your daily cup of coffee, how many stairs you have to walk in your office building, etc.

- A lot of activities involve memorization up to a point. While cooking new recipes you can try to memorize the ingredients and the process of preparing the meal. While learning a new sport (especially with high-coordinative effort) you would also have to remember many things: Coordination, rules, movement, etc.

The bottom line for all these exercises is: Try to use your brain and particularly your memory as often as possible. Many of these activities don't require much extra time, just some extra effort!

CONCLUSION

Memory is a very important part of human life. This book has successfully explained with in-depth examples and instances how important it is that human beings remember as much as possible. It is also evident that the human brain is prone to forgetting, and there are ways one can condition it to remember more, ranging from lifestyle changes to regular exercise to some types of foods that can improve the way you recall things.

It is also important to note that all these tactics are unique to humans, and they are not restricted to just one type of person. We have our own unique makeup and different ways that will work to improve memory. Make sure you identify yours today so that the rate at which you recall things will be significantly improved.

One last thing

If you enjoyed reading this book I would kindly like to ask you to leave a review on Amazon. It'd be greatly appreciated.

www.ingramcontent.com/pod-product-compliance
Lightning Source LLC
Chambersburg PA
CBHW070817220526
45466CB00002B/693